© 2024 by Kaleem Bukhari

All rights reserved. No part of this book may be reproduced, stored in a retrieval system, or transmitted in any form or by any means—electronic, mechanical, photocopying, recording, or otherwise—without prior written permission from the publisher, except for brief quotations embodied in critical reviews and certain other noncommercial uses permitted by copyright law.

The information provided in this book is for educational and informational purposes only. It is not intended to provide legal, financial, or investment advice. The author and publisher disclaim any liability for any actions taken or not taken by readers based on the information contained in this book.

For permission requests, please contact kaleem.bukhari@ymail.com

Chapter 1: Introduction to Cryptocurrency

Understanding the Basics

Evolution of Cryptocurrency

Benefits and Risks

Chapter 2: The Blockchain Revolution

Exploring Blockchain Technology

Decentralization and Security

Applications Beyond Cryptocurrency

Chapter 3: Investing in Cryptocurrency

Getting Started with Crypto Investments

Evaluating Cryptocurrency Projects

Managing Risk and Portfolio Diversification

Chapter 4: Trading Strategies and Techniques

Fundamental Analysis of Cryptocurrencies

Technical Analysis Tools and Indicators

Trading Psychology and Risk Management

Chapter 5: Regulatory Landscape and Compliance

Overview of Cryptocurrency Regulation

Compliance Considerations for Investors and Businesses

Navigating Legal Challenges and Regulatory Uncertainty

Chapter 6: Cryptocurrency Mining and Staking

Introduction to Mining and Staking

Mining Hardware and Software

Staking Protocols and Rewards

Chapter 7: DeFi and the Future of Finance

Understanding Decentralized Finance (DeFi)

Exploring DeFi Protocols and Platforms

Challenges and Opportunities in the DeFi Ecosystem

Chapter 8: Security and Privacy in the Crypto World

Best Practices for Securing Your Crypto Assets

Privacy Coins and Privacy Enhancing Technologies

Protecting Against Scams and Cyber Attacks

The Role of Cryptocurrency in the Global Economy

Cryptocurrency Adoption and Integration

Navigating the Risks and Rewards of Crypto

Assessing Volatility and Market Dynamics

Understanding Black Swan Events and Systemic Risks

Strategies for Thriving in the Crypto Landscape

Conclusion: Embracing the CryptoCraze

Summarising Key Insight

Lessons Learned From Studies and Examples

Exploring Future Trends and Opportunities

Addressing Challenges and Risks

Closing thought and Call to Action.

Chapter One

Introduction to Cryptocurrency: Unveiling the Future of Finance

In the ever-evolving landscape of finance, a revolutionary force has emerged, reshaping the very foundations of how we perceive and transact value – cryptocurrency. Born from the marriage of cutting-edge technology and innovative financial concepts, cryptocurrency has swiftly transcended its status as a mere digital curiosity to become a transformative juggernaut, poised to redefine the global financial landscape.

Defining Cryptocurrency:

At its core, cryptocurrency is a digital or virtual form of currency that employs cryptography for secure financial transactions and decentralized control. Unlike traditional fiat currencies issued by governments, cryptocurrencies operate on decentralized networks built upon blockchain technology – a distributed ledger system that ensures transparency, immutability, and security.

Characteristics of Cryptocurrency:

The hallmark characteristics of cryptocurrency lie in its decentralized nature, cryptographic security, and peer-to-peer transaction model. These attributes endow cryptocurrencies with unparalleled resilience, transparency, and efficiency, fostering trust and facilitating seamless transactions across borders and boundaries.

Evolution of Cryptocurrency:

The journey of cryptocurrency from its humble beginnings to its current status as a global financial disruptor is a testament to the power of innovation and human ingenuity. From the pioneering release of Bitcoin in 2009 by the pseudonymous Satoshi Nakamoto to the proliferation of thousands of alternative cryptocurrencies, the evolution of cryptocurrency has been marked by technological breakthroughs, market fluctuations, and regulatory scrutiny.

Benefits of Cryptocurrency:

Cryptocurrency offers a myriad of benefits to users, investors, and businesses alike. Its decentralized nature eliminates the need for intermediaries, reducing transaction costs and increasing financial inclusion. Cryptocurrencies enable secure, borderless transactions, empower individuals to take control of their financial assets, and foster innovation in payment systems and financial services.

Risks Associated with Cryptocurrency:

However, the meteoric rise of cryptocurrency has also brought forth its share of risks and challenges. Volatility, regulatory uncertainty, security vulnerabilities, and market manipulation are among the risks that investors and users must navigate in the cryptocurrency space. Prudent risk management strategies, regulatory clarity, and technological advancements are essential for mitigating these risks and ensuring the long-term viability of cryptocurrencies.

Impact on the Financial Landscape:

The impact of cryptocurrency on the financial landscape cannot be overstated. From disrupting traditional banking and payment systems to challenging the monopoly of central banks over monetary policy, cryptocurrency is reshaping the very fabric of finance. Its potential to foster financial inclusion, promote economic empowerment, and democratize access to financial services holds the promise of a more equitable and inclusive financial future for all.

In the pages that follow, we will embark on a journey to explore the multifaceted world of cryptocurrency – from its fundamental principles and technological underpinnings to its practical applications, market dynamics, and regulatory challenges. Join us as we delve deeper into the heart of cryptocurrency and uncover the transformative potential that lies at the intersection of technology and finance. Welcome to the future of finance – welcome to the world of cryptocurrency.

Chapter Two

Unveiling the Power of Blockchain: Revolutionizing Decentralization and Security

In the digital age, where data is king and trust is paramount, blockchain technology has emerged as a groundbreaking innovation with the potential to redefine the very fabric of our interconnected world. At its core, blockchain is a distributed ledger technology that enables secure, transparent, and immutable record-keeping of transactions across a decentralized network of computers. Let us embark on a journey to explore the transformative power of blockchain, from its foundational principles to its far-reaching applications beyond the realm of cryptocurrency.

Exploring Blockchain Technology:

At its essence, blockchain is a chain of blocks, where each block contains a cryptographically hashed record of transactions, linked together in a chronological and immutable sequence. This decentralized ledger is maintained and updated by a network of computers, known as nodes, which validate and confirm transactions through a process called consensus.

Decentralization:

The hallmark feature of blockchain is its decentralization, which eliminates the need for a central authority or intermediary to validate and record transactions. Instead, transactions are verified and added to the blockchain by consensus among network participants, ensuring transparency, trust, and resilience in the face of censorship or tampering. Decentralization democratizes access to data and control over assets, empowering individuals and communities to transact peer-to-peer without relying on trusted third parties.

Security:

Blockchain's security is rooted in its cryptographic algorithms and decentralized architecture. Each block in the blockchain is cryptographically linked to the previous block, forming a tamper-evident chain that makes it virtually impossible to alter past transactions without detection. Additionally, blockchain employs consensus mechanisms such as proof of work (PoW) or proof of stake (PoS) to validate transactions and prevent double-spending, further enhancing security and integrity.

Applications Beyond Cryptocurrency:

While blockchain technology gained prominence as the underlying infrastructure for cryptocurrencies like Bitcoin and Ethereum, its potential extends far beyond the realm of digital currencies. Blockchain has found applications in diverse industries and sectors, revolutionizing processes, and unlocking new possibilities for innovation and efficiency.

- **Supply Chain Management:** Blockchain enables transparent and traceable supply chains by recording the provenance and movement of goods from production to distribution. This enhances accountability, reduces fraud, and ensures compliance with regulatory standards, particularly in industries such as food and pharmaceuticals.

- **Identity Management**: Blockchain-based identity management systems provide individuals with greater control over their personal data and digital identities, reducing the risk of identity theft and data breaches. By leveraging decentralized identifiers (DIDs) and verifiable credentials, users can securely manage and share their identity attributes across various platforms and services.

- **Smart Contracts:** Smart contracts are self-executing contracts with the terms of the agreement directly written into code. Deployed on blockchain platforms like Ethereum, smart contracts automate and enforce the execution of contractual agreements, eliminating the need for intermediaries and streamlining processes in areas such as legal contracts, real estate transactions, and supply chain logistics.

- **Digital Voting:** Blockchain-based voting systems offer a secure and transparent alternative to traditional voting methods, enabling verifiable and tamper-proof elections. By recording votes on a blockchain ledger, digital voting systems enhance the integrity and auditability of electoral processes, ensuring fair and democratic outcomes.

In conclusion, blockchain technology represents a paradigm shift in how we conceive of trust, security, and decentralization in the digital age. Its immutable ledger, decentralized architecture, and cryptographic security provide a foundation for innovation across a wide range of industries and applications, from finance and supply chain management to identity verification and governance. As we continue to explore the potential of blockchain technology, we are poised to unlock new opportunities for collaboration, transparency, and empowerment in a rapidly evolving digital landscape. Welcome to the future of trust – welcome to the world of blockchain.

Chapter Three

Embarking on Your Crypto Investment Journey: A Comprehensive Guide

Investing in cryptocurrencies has emerged as a compelling opportunity for investors seeking exposure to the digital assets market and the potential for high returns. However, navigating the complexities of crypto investing requires careful consideration of various factors, including getting started, evaluating crypto projects, and managing risk through portfolio diversification. Let's delve into each aspect in-depth to equip you with the knowledge and insights needed to embark on your crypto investment journey.

Getting Started with Crypto Investment:

1. Educate Yourself: Before diving into crypto investing, it's essential to educate yourself about the fundamentals of cryptocurrencies, blockchain technology, and the dynamics of the crypto market. Resources such as books, online courses, forums, and reputable websites can provide valuable insights and guidance for beginners.

2. Understand the Risks: Crypto investing carries inherent risks, including market volatility, regulatory uncertainty, security vulnerabilities, and technological risks. It's crucial to understand these risks and be prepared to handle them effectively through risk management strategies.

3. Choose a Reliable Exchange: Selecting a reputable cryptocurrency exchange is essential for buying, selling, and trading cryptocurrencies securely. Look for exchanges with robust security measures, regulatory compliance, user-friendly interfaces, and a diverse range of supported assets.

4. Secure Your Investments: Protecting your crypto assets from theft, hacking, and unauthorized access is paramount. Use hardware wallets or secure cold storage solutions to store your cryptocurrencies offline, enable two-factor authentication (2FA) for added security, and practice good password hygiene.

Evaluating Crypto Projects:

1. Research and Due Diligence: Conduct thorough research and due diligence before investing in any cryptocurrency project. Evaluate factors such as the team's credentials and experience, the project's technological innovation and utility, its market potential and adoption, and its competitive landscape.

2. Review Whitepapers and Roadmaps: Read the project's whitepaper and roadmap to understand its vision, objectives, technical specifications, and development milestones. Look for transparency, clarity, and credibility in the project's documentation and communication channels.

3. Assess Community and Ecosystem: Evaluate the strength and engagement of the project's community and ecosystem, including its social media presence, online forums, developer activity, and partnerships. A vibrant and supportive community can indicate confidence and momentum behind the project.

4. Consider Tokenomics and Economics: Analyze the tokenomics and economics of the cryptocurrency project, including its token distribution, supply dynamics, inflationary or deflationary mechanisms, and potential for utility and value accrual over time.

Risk Management and Portfolio Diversification:

1. Diversify Your Portfolio: Diversification is key to managing risk and reducing exposure to individual assets or market sectors. Allocate your investment across a diverse range of cryptocurrencies, asset classes, and investment strategies to mitigate concentration risk and optimize risk-adjusted returns.

2. Set Investment Goals and Risk Tolerance: Define your investment goals, time horizon, and risk tolerance before building your crypto portfolio. Determine whether you're investing for short-term speculation, long-term growth, income generation, or hedging against inflation and market volatility.

3. Manage Position Sizes: Manage your position sizes and allocation percentages based on your risk tolerance, investment goals, and market conditions. Avoid overexposure to high-risk assets or speculative projects, and rebalance your portfolio periodically to maintain optimal asset allocation.

4. Stay Informed and Adaptive: Stay informed about market developments, industry trends, and regulatory changes that may impact your crypto investments. Be adaptive and open to adjusting your investment strategy based on new information, market dynamics, and evolving opportunities and risks.

In conclusion, investing in cryptocurrencies offers unique opportunities for investors to participate in the growth and innovation of the digital economy. By getting started with crypto investment, evaluating crypto projects effectively, and managing risk through portfolio diversification, investors can navigate the complexities of the crypto market and potentially reap the rewards of this dynamic and evolving asset class. Remember to stay informed, remain vigilant, and approach crypto investing with a disciplined and long-term perspective.

Mastering Crypto Trading: A Comprehensive Guide to Strategies, Techniques, and Psychology

Trading cryptocurrencies presents a dynamic and ever-evolving landscape, requiring traders to navigate through a multitude of strategies, techniques, and psychological considerations. In this comprehensive guide, we'll explore fundamental analysis, technical analysis, trading strategies, tactics, and the critical aspects of trading psychology and risk management essential for success in the crypto markets.

Fundamental Analysis of Cryptocurrency:

1. Understanding the Basics: Fundamental analysis involves evaluating the intrinsic value of a cryptocurrency based on factors such as its technology, team, community, adoption, and market potential.

2. Research and Due Diligence: Conduct thorough research and due diligence on the cryptocurrency project, including its whitepaper, team members, partnerships, use cases, and competitive advantages.

3. Market Sentiment and News Analysis: Monitor market sentiment and news developments that may impact the price and perception of the cryptocurrency. Factors such as regulatory announcements, technological advancements, and macroeconomic trends can influence market sentiment.

Technical Analysis and Indicators:

1. Chart Analysis: Technical analysis involves analyzing price charts and patterns to identify trends, support and resistance levels, and potential entry and exit points for trades.

2. Common Technical Indicators: Utilize a variety of technical indicators such as moving averages, relative strength index (RSI), stochastic oscillator, MACD, and Bollinger Bands to identify overbought or oversold conditions, trend reversals, and trading opportunities.

3. Candlestick Patterns: Learn to interpret candlestick patterns, such as bullish engulfing, bearish engulfing, doji, hammer, and shooting star, to gauge market sentiment and predict price movements.

Trading Strategies and Tactics:

1. Trend Following: The trend-following strategy involves identifying and riding trends in the market by buying assets in uptrends and selling in downtrends. Use technical indicators such as moving averages and trendlines to confirm trend direction and momentum.

2. Range Trading: Range trading involves buying at support levels and selling at resistance levels within a defined price range. Identify key support and resistance levels using chart patterns and technical analysis tools and execute trades accordingly.

3. Breakout Trading: Breakout trading involves entering trades when the price breaks out of a consolidation phase or a significant support or resistance level. Use volume analysis, volatility indicators, and chart patterns to confirm breakouts and capitalize on price momentum.

4. Scalping and Day Trading: Scalping and day trading involve executing short-term trades to capitalize on small price movements throughout the day. Use technical analysis tools, order flow analysis, and fast execution

platforms to identify and execute trades quickly.

Trading Psychology and Risk Management:

1. **Emotional Discipline:** Develop emotional discipline and resilience to manage fear, greed, FOMO (fear of missing out), and FUD (fear, uncertainty, and doubt). Stick to your trading plan, maintain a long-term perspective, and avoid making impulsive decisions based on emotions.

2. **Risk Management:** Implement robust risk management strategies to protect your capital and minimize losses. Determine your risk tolerance, set stop-loss orders to limit losses, and never risk more than you can afford to lose on any single trade.

3. **Position Sizing:** Proper position sizing is essential for managing risk and maximizing returns. Determine the appropriate position size based on your risk tolerance, account size, and the probability of success of the trade.

4. Continuous Learning and Improvement: Stay informed about market developments, trading techniques, and psychological strategies through continuous learning and self-improvement. Keep a trading journal to track your trades, analyze your performance, and identify areas for improvement.

In conclusion, mastering crypto trading requires a combination of technical expertise, analytical skills, emotional discipline, and risk management techniques. By integrating fundamental analysis, technical analysis, trading strategies, tactics, and trading psychology into your trading approach, you can increase your chances of success and achieve your financial goals in the dynamic and competitive world of cryptocurrency trading. Remember to stay patient, disciplined, and adaptable, and never stop learning and evolving as a trader.

Chapter Five

Navigating the Regulatory Landscape: Cryptocurrency Compliance and Legal Considerations

In the fast-paced world of cryptocurrency, navigating the regulatory landscape is essential for investors and businesses alike to ensure compliance, mitigate risks, and navigate legal challenges and uncertainties. This detailed guide provides an overview of the regulatory landscape surrounding cryptocurrency, compliance considerations for investors and businesses, and strategies for navigating legal challenges and regulatory uncertainties.

Overview of Cryptocurrency Regulation:

1. Global Regulatory Landscape: Cryptocurrency regulation varies significantly from country to country, with some jurisdictions embracing cryptocurrencies and blockchain technology, while others adopt a more cautious or restrictive approach. Regulatory frameworks may encompass securities laws, anti-money laundering (AML) and know-your-customer (KYC) regulations, tax laws, and consumer protection measures.

2. Regulatory Bodies: Regulatory oversight of cryptocurrencies may fall under the jurisdiction of government agencies such as financial regulatory authorities, central banks, securities commissions, tax authorities, and law enforcement agencies. International organizations such as the Financial Action Task Force (FATF) also provide guidelines and recommendations for combating money laundering and terrorist financing involving cryptocurrencies.

Compliance Considerations for Investors:

1. Know-Your-Customer (KYC) and Anti-Money Laundering (AML) Requirements: Many cryptocurrency exchanges and trading platforms require users to undergo KYC verification procedures to comply with AML regulations. Investors may need to provide identification documents, proof of address, and other information to verify their identity and source of funds.

2. Tax Compliance: Cryptocurrency transactions may be subject to tax obligations, including capital gains tax, income tax, and transactional taxes such as value-added tax (VAT). Investors should familiarize themselves with

tax regulations in their jurisdiction and maintain accurate records of their cryptocurrency transactions for tax reporting purposes.

3. Security and Custody: Security is paramount in cryptocurrency investing, as investors are responsible for safeguarding their digital assets from theft, hacking, and unauthorized access. Use secure hardware wallets or reputable custodial services to store cryptocurrency assets securely and implement best practices for password management and account security.

Compliance Considerations for Businesses:

1. Regulatory Licensing and Registration: Businesses operating in the cryptocurrency industry may be required to obtain licenses or register with regulatory authorities, depending on the nature of their activities. This may include cryptocurrency exchanges, wallet providers, payment processors, and other service providers.

2. Compliance Policies and Procedures: Implement robust compliance policies and procedures to ensure adherence to regulatory requirements, including KYC/AML

procedures, transaction monitoring, suspicious activity reporting, and customer due diligence. Conduct regular audits and reviews to assess compliance with regulatory standards and address any deficiencies or gaps.

3. Risk Management and Legal Counsel: Develop risk management strategies to mitigate legal and regulatory risks associated with cryptocurrency operations, such as regulatory uncertainty, enforcement actions, litigation, and reputational damage. Seek advice from legal counsel with expertise in cryptocurrency law to navigate complex legal issues and regulatory challenges effectively.

Navigating Legal Challenges and Regulatory Uncertainty:

1. Engage with Regulators: Foster open communication and engagement with regulatory authorities to stay informed about regulatory developments, seek guidance on compliance requirements, and advocate for clear and balanced regulations that support innovation while protecting investors and consumers.

2. Monitor Regulatory Developments: Stay abreast of regulatory developments and legislative changes that may impact the cryptocurrency industry, both domestically and internationally. Monitor regulatory announcements, policy proposals, enforcement actions, and court rulings to assess their implications for your business or investment strategy.

3. Adaptability and Flexibility: Cryptocurrency regulation is a rapidly evolving and dynamic field, requiring businesses and investors to remain adaptable and flexible in response to regulatory changes and market developments. Develop contingency plans and risk mitigation strategies to adjust your operations or investment approach in light of changing regulatory environments or legal uncertainties.

In conclusion, navigating the regulatory landscape and ensuring compliance with legal requirements are essential for investors and businesses operating in the cryptocurrency industry. By understanding the regulatory framework, implementing robust compliance measures, and staying vigilant about legal challenges and regulatory uncertainties, stakeholders can mitigate risks, foster trust and confidence, and contribute to the long-term growth and sustainability of the cryptocurrency ecosystem. Remember to seek professional advice and legal counsel when necessary and to prioritize compliance and regulatory adherence in all aspects of cryptocurrency investing and business operations.

Chapter Six

Unveiling the World of Crypto Mining and Staking: A Comprehensive Guide

In the realm of cryptocurrencies, two fundamental processes play a vital role in securing blockchain networks and validating transactions: mining and staking. In this comprehensive guide, we will delve into the intricacies of crypto mining and staking, exploring their respective concepts, hardware and software requirements, protocols, rewards systems, and a comparative analysis of their advantages and limitations.

Introduction to Mining and Staking:

1. Mining: Crypto mining is the process of validating and adding new transactions to a blockchain ledger through computational work. Miners compete to solve complex mathematical puzzles, known as cryptographic hashes, to validate transactions and create new blocks in the blockchain. In return for their efforts, miners are rewarded with newly minted cryptocurrency tokens and transaction fees.

2. Staking: Staking, on the other hand, is a consensus mechanism that relies on participants, known as validators or stakers, to validate transactions and secure the blockchain network. Instead of solving computational puzzles, stakers lock up a certain amount of cryptocurrency tokens as collateral, known as a stake, to participate in the validation process. Validators are selected to create new blocks and validate transactions based on the size of their stake and other factors determined by the staking protocol.

Mining Hardware and Software:

1. Hardware: Mining hardware plays a crucial role in the efficiency and profitability of crypto mining operations. Specialized mining hardware, known as application-specific integrated circuits (ASICs), are designed to perform the computational calculations required for mining with optimal efficiency. Popular mining algorithms such as SHA-256 (used by Bitcoin) and Ethash (used by Ethereum) require specific ASIC miners for optimal performance.

2. Software: Mining software is used to configure and control mining hardware, connect to mining pools (groups of miners who collaborate to increase their chances of earning rewards), and monitor mining performance. Popular mining software includes CGMiner, BFGMiner, and NiceHash for Bitcoin mining, and Claymore's Dual Miner and PhoenixMiner for Ethereum mining.

Staking Protocols and Rewards:

1. Proof-of-Stake (PoS): PoS is a staking protocol that selects validators to create new blocks and validate transactions based on the amount of cryptocurrency tokens they hold as collateral (stake) and other factors such as reputation and network age. Validators are rewarded with transaction fees and newly minted tokens proportional to their stake.

2. Delegated Proof-of-Stake (DPoS): DPoS is a variation of the PoS consensus mechanism where token holders vote for delegates to represent them as validators. Delegates are responsible for creating new blocks and validating transactions on behalf of token holders. Delegates are rewarded with transaction fees and block

rewards for their services.

3. Proof-of-Work (PoW) vs. Proof-of-Stake (PoS): PoW and PoS are two distinct consensus mechanisms with their own advantages and limitations. PoW requires significant computational resources and energy consumption but provides a high level of security and decentralization. PoS is more energy-efficient and scalable but may be susceptible to certain attack vectors such as the "nothing-at-stake" problem and long-range attacks.

Comparing Staking and Mining:

1. Resource Requirements: Mining requires specialized hardware (ASICs) and consumes a significant amount of electricity, while staking requires cryptocurrency tokens as collateral but is more energy-efficient and environmentally friendly.

2. Security and Decentralization: PoW mining provides a high level of security and decentralization due to its resource-intensive nature, while PoS may be more susceptible to centralization risks if a small number of validators control a significant portion of the stake.

3. Rewards and Incentives: Miners are rewarded with newly minted cryptocurrency tokens and transaction fees for their mining efforts, while stakers earn rewards in the form of transaction fees and block rewards proportional to their stake.

4. Flexibility and Accessibility: Staking offers greater accessibility and participation opportunities for cryptocurrency holders with any amount of tokens, while mining requires substantial upfront investment in hardware and operational costs.

In conclusion, crypto mining and staking are essential processes that contribute to the security, decentralization, and functionality of blockchain networks. While mining relies on computational work and specialized hardware, staking leverages token ownership and collateral to validate transactions and secure the network. Understanding the differences, advantages, and limitations of mining and staking can help investors and participants make informed decisions about their involvement in the cryptocurrency ecosystem.

Chapter Seven

Unveiling the Future of Finance: Understanding Decentralized Finance (DeFi)

In recent years, decentralized finance (DeFi) has emerged as a transformative force in the financial industry, offering a paradigm shift from traditional centralized systems to open, permissionless, and trustless protocols built on blockchain technology. In this professional explanation, we will explore the concept of decentralized finance, delve into DeFi protocols and platforms, discuss the challenges and opportunities within the DeFi ecosystem, and highlight real-world case studies and use cases driving innovation in the future of finance.

Understanding Decentralized Finance (DeFi):

1. Concept and Principles: Decentralized finance, or DeFi, refers to a broad category of financial services and applications that operate on decentralized networks, such as Ethereum, and utilize smart contracts to automate and execute financial transactions without the need for intermediaries. DeFi aims to democratize access to financial services, increase financial inclusion, and

eliminate barriers to participation in the global economy.

2. Key Principles: DeFi is characterized by several key principles, including decentralization, interoperability, transparency, programmability, and censorship resistance. These principles enable open access, permissionless innovation, and trustless transactions in the DeFi ecosystem, empowering individuals to control their financial assets and participate in peer-to-peer lending, borrowing, trading, and other financial activities.

Exploring DeFi Protocols and Platforms:

1. Decentralized Exchanges (DEXs): Decentralized exchanges facilitate peer-to-peer trading of digital assets without relying oncentralized intermediaries. DEXs leverage automated market makers (AMMs) and liquidity pools to enable seamless and trustless trading of cryptocurrencies and tokens.

2. Lending and Borrowing Protocols : DeFi lending platforms allow users to lend their cryptocurrency assets to earn interest or borrow assets against collateralized positions. Smart contract-based lending protocols, such

as Compound and Aave, enable users to access liquidity and earn yields on their idle assets.

3. Stablecoins and Payment Networks: Stablecoins are cryptocurrencies pegged to fiat currencies or other stable assets, providing stability and utility for DeFi transactions. Payment networks, such as MakerDAO and Terra, facilitate the issuance and use of stablecoins for peer-to-peer payments, remittances, and decentralized finance applications.

Challenges and Opportunities in the DeFi Ecosystem:

1. Scalability and User Experience: Scalability remains a significant challenge for DeFi platforms, as blockchain networks face limitations in transaction throughput and latency. Improving user experience and onboarding processes is essential for mainstream adoption of DeFi applications.

2. Security and Auditing: DeFi platforms are susceptible to smart contract bugs, vulnerabilities, and security exploits, posing risks to user funds and platform integrity. Conducting comprehensive security audits, implementing best practices for smart contract development, and enhancing security measures are critical for mitigating risks in the DeFi ecosystem.

3. Regulatory Compliance: Regulatory uncertainty and compliance requirements present challenges for DeFi platforms, particularly regarding know-your-customer (KYC) and anti-money laundering (AML) regulations. Collaborating with regulatory authorities, adopting compliance frameworks, and promoting transparency are essential for addressing regulatory concerns and fostering trust in the DeFi ecosystem.

Case Studies and Use Cases:

1. Decentralized Lending: Platforms like Compound and Aave enable users to lend and borrow digital assets in a decentralized and permissionless manner, providing access to liquidity and earning yields on deposited assets.

2. Automated Market Making: Decentralized exchanges such as Uniswap and SushiSwap leverage automated market maker (AMM) algorithms to provide liquidity for trading pairs and enable seamless token swaps without order books or centralized intermediaries.

3. Tokenization of Assets: Projects like Synthetix and Mirror Protocol enable the tokenization of real-world assets, such as stocks, commodities, and fiat currencies, allowing users to trade synthetic assets and gain exposure to traditional financial markets within the DeFi ecosystem.

In conclusion, decentralized finance (DeFi) represents a paradigm shift in the way financial services are accessed, executed, and experienced. By leveraging blockchain technology, smart contracts, and decentralized networks, DeFi platforms offer innovative solutions to traditional financial challenges, while also presenting new opportunities and risks for users and participants. As the DeFi ecosystem continues to evolve and mature, collaboration, innovation, and responsible stewardship will be essential for realizing the full potential of decentralized finance in shaping the future of finance.

Chapter Eight

Safeguarding Your Crypto Assets: A Comprehensive Guide to Security and Privacy

In the dynamic world of cryptocurrencies, security and privacy are paramount considerations for safeguarding your valuable assets from threats such as theft, fraud, and unauthorized access. In this expressive explanation, we will explore best practices for securing your crypto assets, privacy-enhancing technologies, protection against scams and cyber attacks, and regulatory compliance and reporting obligations to ensure the safety and privacy of your digital wealth.

Best Practices for Securing Your Crypto Assets:

1. Use Secure Wallets: Choose reputable and secure cryptocurrency wallets to store your digital assets. Hardware wallets, such as Ledger and Trezor, offer enhanced security by storing your private keys offline and protecting them from hacking and malware attacks.

2. Implement Strong Passwords: Use strong, unique passwords for your crypto accounts and wallets to prevent unauthorized access. Enable two-factor authentication (2FA) whenever possible to add an extra layer of security to your accounts.

3. Backup Your Keys: Backup your wallet's private keys or recovery seed phrase in multiple secure locations, such as encrypted USB drives or physical paper wallets. Ensure that your backup is stored offline and inaccessible to unauthorized individuals.

4. Update Software Regularly: Keep your cryptocurrency wallets, software, and operating systems up-to-date with the latest security patches and updates to protect against known vulnerabilities and exploits.

Privacy Coins and Privacy-Enhancing Technology:

1. Privacy Coins: Privacy coins such as Monero (XMR), Zcash (ZEC), and Dash (DASH) are designed to provide enhanced privacy and anonymity for cryptocurrency

transactions. These coins utilize cryptographic techniques such as ring signatures, zk-SNARKs, and CoinJoin to obfuscate transaction details and protect user privacy.

2. Privacy-Enhancing Tools: Utilize privacy-enhancing tools and technologies, such as VPNs (virtual private networks), Tor (The Onion Router), and encrypted messaging apps, to protect your online activities and communications from surveillance and monitoring.

Protection Against Scams and Cyber Attacks:

1. Exercise Caution: Be cautious of phishing scams, fraudulent schemes, and social engineering tactics used by malicious actors to steal your cryptocurrency. Verify the authenticity of websites, emails, and messages before providing sensitive information or making transactions.

2. Secure Your Communications: Use end-to-end encrypted messaging apps, such as Signal or Telegram, to protect your communications from interception and eavesdropping. Avoid sharing sensitive information or

private keys over unsecured channels.

3. Stay Informed: Stay informed about common scams and cyber threats targeting cryptocurrency users, such as fake ICOs (initial coin offerings), Ponzi schemes, and ransomware attacks. Educate yourself about warning signs and best practices for identifying and avoiding potential scams.

Regulatory Compliance and Reporting Obligations:

1. Know Your Responsibilities: Familiarize yourself with regulatory requirements and reporting obligations related to cryptocurrency transactions in your jurisdiction. Understand your tax obligations, anti-money laundering (AML) requirements, and reporting obligations for cryptocurrency gains and transactions.

2. Keep Accurate Records: Maintain accurate records of your cryptocurrency transactions, including buy and sell orders, withdrawals and deposits, and trading activity. Keep receipts, invoices, and documentation to support your tax reporting and compliance efforts.

3. Report Suspicious Activity: Report any suspicious activity or potential security breaches to the relevant authorities, exchanges, or regulatory agencies. Cooperate with law enforcement investigations and follow reporting procedures outlined by your cryptocurrency service providers.

In conclusion, security and privacy are essential considerations for protecting your crypto assets and preserving your financial autonomy in the digital age. By implementing best practices for securing your crypto assets, leveraging privacy-enhancing technologies, staying vigilant against scams and cyber attacks, and complying with regulatory requirements, you can safeguard your digital wealth and enjoy the benefits of cryptocurrency ownership with confidence and peace of mind.

Chapter Nine

Cryptocurrency's Role in Financial Institutions: A Deep Exploration

Cryptocurrency's emergence has significantly impacted the traditional financial landscape, offering both opportunities and challenges for financial institutions worldwide. In this deep explanation, we will delve into the roles of cryptocurrency in financial institutions, focusing on adoption and integration, implications for traditional financial institutions, future trends and predictions, as well as the challenges and opportunities associated with navigating the risks and rewards of cryptocurrency.

Crypto Adoption and Integration:

1. Adoption by Financial Institutions: Increasingly, financial institutions are recognizing the potential of cryptocurrencies and blockchain technology. Many banks, investment firms, and payment processors are exploring crypto adoption and integration into their operations, offering cryptocurrency custody services, facilitating crypto trading for clients, and investing in blockchain-based solutions.

2. Integration into Financial Products: Cryptocurrencies are being integrated into a wide range of financial products and services, including investment funds, exchange-traded products (ETPs), derivatives, and payment solutions. Crypto-backed loans, interest-bearing accounts, and decentralized finance (DeFi) platforms are also gaining traction, providing new avenues for accessing capital and earning yields.

Implications for Traditional Financial Institutions:

1. Disruption of Traditional Banking: Cryptocurrencies and blockchain technology pose a disruptive threat to traditional banking models, potentially bypassing intermediaries and reducing the need for traditional financial services such as remittances, cross-border payments, and lending.

2. Competition and Innovation: Traditional financial institutions face competition from crypto-native firms and startups offering innovative financial products and services. The rise of decentralized finance (DeFi) platforms and non-bank digital asset exchanges

challenges traditional business models and forces incumbents to adapt or risk becoming obsolete.

Future Trends and Predictions:

1. Mainstream Adoption: Despite regulatory challenges and market volatility, mainstream adoption of cryptocurrencies is expected to continue growing, driven by increasing institutional interest, technological advancements, and evolving consumer preferences.

2. Regulatory Clarity: Regulatory frameworks governing cryptocurrencies and blockchain technology are expected to evolve to provide greater clarity and certainty for market participants. Regulatory oversight and compliance requirements may increase, particularly for financial institutions offering crypto-related services.

Challenges and Opportunities:

1. Regulatory Uncertainty: Regulatory uncertainty remains a significant challenge for financial institutions navigating the cryptocurrency landscape. Ambiguous or conflicting

regulations across jurisdictions create compliance risks and legal uncertainties, requiring financial institutions to carefully assess and mitigate regulatory risks.

2. Security and Custody: Security concerns surrounding cryptocurrency custody, storage, and management pose risks for financial institutions, particularly in light of high-profile hacks and security breaches. Implementing robust security measures, such as multi-signature wallets, cold storage solutions, and rigorous security protocols, is essential for safeguarding crypto assets.

Navigating the Risks and Rewards of Cryptocurrency:

1. Risk Management: Financial institutions must develop comprehensive risk management strategies to address the unique risks associated with cryptocurrency, including market volatility, regulatory compliance, operational risks, and cybersecurity threats. Implementing robust risk controls, conducting thorough due diligence, and staying informed about market developments are critical for managing risk effectively.

2. Opportunities for Innovation: Despite the challenges, cryptocurrencies offer significant opportunities for innovation and growth in the financial industry. Financial institutions can leverage blockchain technology to streamline operations, reduce costs, enhance transparency, and improve financial inclusion, ultimately driving greater efficiency and value for their clients.

In conclusion, cryptocurrency's role in financial institutions is evolving rapidly, presenting both opportunities and challenges for incumbents and newcomers alike. By embracing crypto adoption and integration, anticipating future trends, navigating regulatory complexities, and implementing robust risk management strategies, financial institutions can position themselves to thrive in the digital economy and harness the transformative potential of cryptocurrencies for the benefit of their clients and stakeholders.

Chapter Ten

Navigating Risk and Rewards in Cryptocurrency: A Comprehensive Guide

Cryptocurrency investment and trading present a unique blend of risks and rewards, requiring careful navigation and strategic decision-making to achieve success in this dynamic and volatile market. In this thorough explanation, we will explore the key aspects of navigating risk and rewards in cryptocurrency, including assessing volatility and market dynamics, understanding black swan events and systematic risk, strategies for thriving in the crypto landscape, and the psychological aspects of crypto investing and trading.

Assessing Volatility and Market Dynamics:

1. Volatility: Cryptocurrency markets are known for their high volatility, with prices often experiencing significant fluctuations within short time frames. While volatility can create opportunities for profit, it also increases the risk of losses and requires investors and traders to manage their positions prudently.

2. Market Dynamics: Understanding market dynamics, including supply and demand factors, investor sentiment, macroeconomic trends, and technological developments, is essential for making informed investment decisions and navigating market volatility effectively. Technical analysis, fundamental analysis, and sentiment analysis can help identify trends and patterns in cryptocurrency markets.

Understanding Black Swan Events and Systematic Risk:

1. Black Swan Events: Black swan events refer to unexpected and rare events with severe and widespread consequences, such as regulatory crackdowns, security breaches, market manipulation, or geopolitical crises, that can disrupt cryptocurrency markets and cause significant losses for investors.

2. Systematic Risk: Systematic risk, also known as market risk, refers to the inherent risk of investing in the broader cryptocurrency market, including factors such as market sentiment, macroeconomic conditions, regulatory changes, and technological risks that can affect all cryptocurrencies simultaneously.

Strategies for Thriving in the Crypto Landscape:

1. Diversification: Diversifying your cryptocurrency portfolio across multiple assets, sectors, and investment strategies can help mitigate risk and reduce exposure to individual asset volatility. Consider allocating a portion of your portfolio to different types of cryptocurrencies, including established coins, emerging projects, and decentralized finance (DeFi) tokens.

2. Risk Management: Implement robust risk management strategies, including setting stop-loss orders, defining risk-reward ratios, and allocating capital prudently based on your risk tolerance and investment objectives. Avoid investing more than you can afford to lose and maintain a long-term perspective to ride out market fluctuations.

3. Continuous Learning: Stay informed about the latest developments, trends, and news in the cryptocurrency space through continuous learning and research. Follow reputable sources, participate in online communities, attend conferences and events, and engage with experienced investors and traders to expand your knowledge and stay ahead of market trends.

Psychological Aspects of Crypto Investing and Trading:

1. Emotional Discipline: Develop emotional discipline and resilience to avoid making impulsive decisions based on fear, greed, or FOMO (fear of missing out). Stick to your trading plan, maintain a rational mindset, and avoid letting emotions dictate your investment strategy.

2. Patience and Persistence: Cryptocurrency investing and trading require patience and persistence to navigate market volatility and achieve long-term success. Focus on consistency, discipline, and continuous improvement, rather than chasing short-term gains or trying to time the market.

3. Risk Awareness: Be aware of the psychological biases and cognitive errors that can influence decision-making in cryptocurrency investing and trading, such as overconfidence, confirmation bias, and herd mentality. Stay vigilant, challenge your assumptions, and maintain a healthy skepticism to avoid falling prey to common pitfalls and traps in the market.

In conclusion, navigating risk and rewards in cryptocurrency requires a combination of strategic planning, risk management, continuous learning, and emotional discipline. By assessing volatility and market dynamics, understanding black swan events and systematic risk, implementing effective strategies for thriving in the crypto landscape, and being mindful of the psychological aspects of investing and trading, investors and traders can increase their chances of success and achieve their financial goals in this exciting and evolving market.

Chapter Eleven

Concluding Cryptocraze: Embracing the Future of Finance

In the journey through Cryptocraze, we've embarked on an exploration of the transformative power of cryptocurrency and blockchain technology in shaping the future of finance. As we reach the conclusion of this book, let's reflect on the key insights, lessons learned, future trends, opportunities, challenges, and risks that define the crypto landscape, and consider the implications for individuals, businesses, and society as a whole.

Summarizing Key Insights:

Throughout Cryptocraze, we've uncovered the revolutionary potential of cryptocurrencies to democratize access to financial services, empower individuals with greater financial autonomy, and drive innovation in the global economy. From decentralized finance (DeFi) platforms to non-fungible tokens (NFTs), blockchain-based applications are redefining traditional paradigms and unlocking new possibilities for collaboration, creativity, and value creation.

Lessons Learned from Case Studies and Examples:

Case studies and examples have illuminated the real-world applications and use cases of cryptocurrencies, from remittances and cross-border payments to decentralized autonomous organizations (DAOs) and tokenized assets. We've learned from the successes and failures of past projects, gaining valuable insights into the importance of innovation, resilience, and adaptability in navigating the complex and evolving crypto landscape.

Exploring Future Trends and Opportunities:

Looking ahead, the future of cryptocurrency is brimming with potential, driven by emerging trends such as institutional adoption, regulatory clarity, technological advancements, and mainstream acceptance. Opportunities abound for entrepreneurs, investors, and innovators to capitalize on the growing demand for crypto-based solutions and contribute to the ongoing evolution of the digital economy.

Addressing Challenges and Risks:

Despite its promise, the crypto landscape is not without its challenges and risks. Volatility, regulatory uncertainty, security concerns, and market manipulation pose significant hurdles for market participants, requiring vigilance, resilience, and risk management strategies to navigate successfully. By addressing these challenges head-on and fostering collaboration and cooperation within the industry, we can overcome obstacles and unlock the full potential of cryptocurrencies and blockchain technology.

Closing Thoughts and Call to Action:

As we conclude our journey through Cryptocraze, let us embrace the opportunities and challenges that lie ahead with optimism, determination, and a spirit of innovation. Whether you're an investor seeking alpha, an entrepreneur building the next killer app, or an enthusiast exploring the frontiers of decentralized finance, remember that the crypto revolution is just beginning, and the possibilities are limitless. Together, let's shape the future of finance and build a more inclusive, transparent, and resilient financial ecosystem for generations to come.

In closing, I invite you to continue your exploration of cryptocurrencies and blockchain technology, to stay informed, to engage with the community, and to seize the opportunities that await in this brave new world of finance. Cryptocraze may be ending, but the journey is far from over. Embrace the future, embrace the possibilities, and together, let's make history in the Cryptocurrency Craze.

www.ingramcontent.com/pod-product-compliance
Lightning Source LLC
Chambersburg PA
CBHW071548240526
45470CB00023B/2073